COMMUNITY HELPERS

Bus Drivers

by Mari Schuh

BELLWETHER MEDIA • MINNEAPOLIS, MN

Note to Librarians, Teachers, and Parents:

Blastoff! Readers are carefully developed by literacy experts and combine standards-based content with developmentally appropriate text.

Level 1 provides the most support through repetition of high-frequency words, light text, predictable sentence patterns, and strong visual support.

Level 2 offers early readers a bit more challenge through varied simple sentences, increased text load, and less repetition of high-frequency words.

Level 3 advances early-fluent readers toward fluency through increased text and concept load, less reliance on visuals, longer sentences, and more literary language.

Level 4 builds reading stamina by providing more text per page, increased use of punctuation, greater variation in sentence patterns, and increasingly challenging vocabulary.

Level 5 encourages children to move from "learning to read" to "reading to learn" by providing even more text, varied writing styles, and less familiar topics.

Whichever book is right for your reader, Blastoff! Readers are the perfect books to build confidence and encourage a love of reading that will last a lifetime!

This edition first published in 2018 by Bellwether Media, Inc.

No part of this publication may be reproduced in whole or in part without written permission of the publisher. For information regarding permission, write to Bellwether Media, Inc., Attention: Permissions Department, 5357 Penn Avenue South, Minneapolis, MN 55419.

Library of Congress Cataloging-in-Publication Data

Names: Schuh, Mari C., 1975- author.
Title: Bus Drivers / by Mari Schuh.
Description: Minneapolis, MN : Bellwether Media, Inc., [2018] | Series: Blastoff! Readers. Community Helpers |
   Includes bibliographical references and index. | Audience: Ages 5-8. | Audience: Grades K to 3.
Identifiers: LCCN 2017032990 (print) | LCCN 2017035700 (ebook) | ISBN
   9781626177420 (hardcover : alk. paper) | ISBN 9781681034997 (ebook)
Subjects: LCSH: Bus driving–Juvenile literature. | Bus drivers–Juvenile
   literature. | Transportation, Automotive–Juvenile literature.
Classification: LCC TL232.3 (ebook) | LCC TL232.3 .S38 2018 (print) | DDC 629.28/333–dc23
LC record available at https://lccn.loc.gov/2017032990

Editor: Nathan Sommer   Designer: Brittany McIntosh

Printed in the United States of America, North Mankato, MN.

Table of Contents

At the Bus Stop	4
What Are Bus Drivers?	8
What Do Bus Drivers Do?	12
What Makes a Good Bus Driver?	18
Glossary	22
To Learn More	23
Index	24

Today is Diana's first bus ride. She is nervous. The bus driver says hi!

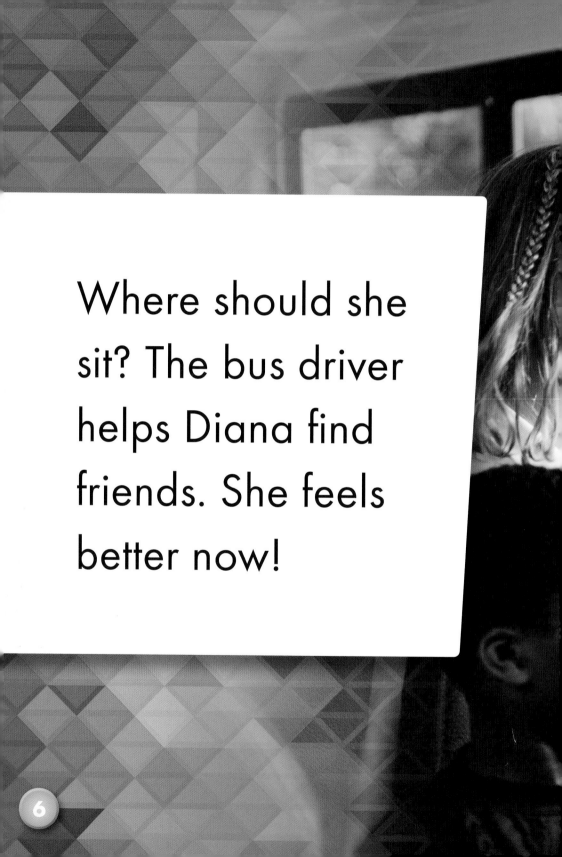

Where should she sit? The bus driver helps Diana find friends. She feels better now!

EMERGENCY EXIT
SORTIE DE SECOURS

What Are Bus Drivers?

Bus drivers drive buses from place to place. They work in small towns and big cities.

Bus drivers get people to school and work. Some drive on **tours** or **field trips**.

tour bus 11

What Do Bus Drivers Do?

Bus drivers keep **passengers** safe. They follow all **traffic laws**.

Bus Driver Gear

steering wheel   **lights**   **sunglasses**   **stop sign**

These helpers drive the same **route** daily. Many gather **fares** from passengers.

passenger paying fare

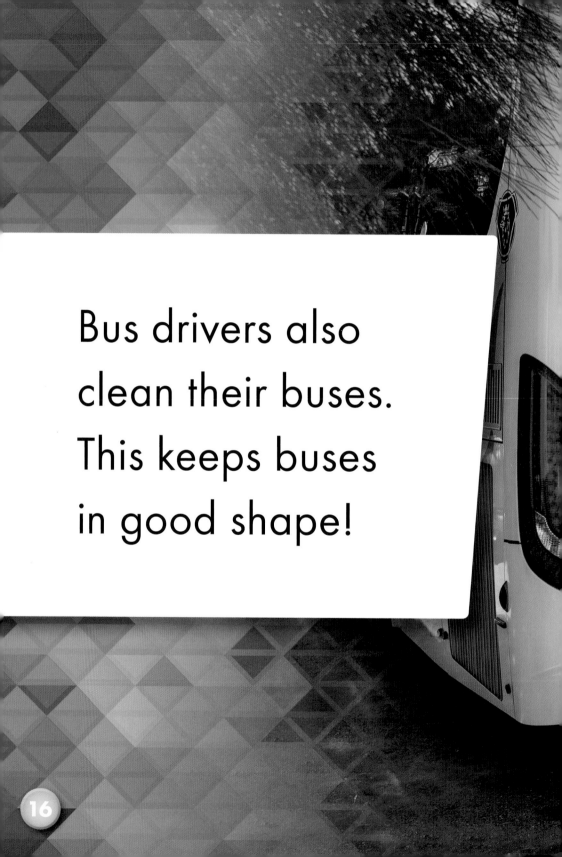

Bus drivers also
clean their buses.
This keeps buses
in good shape!

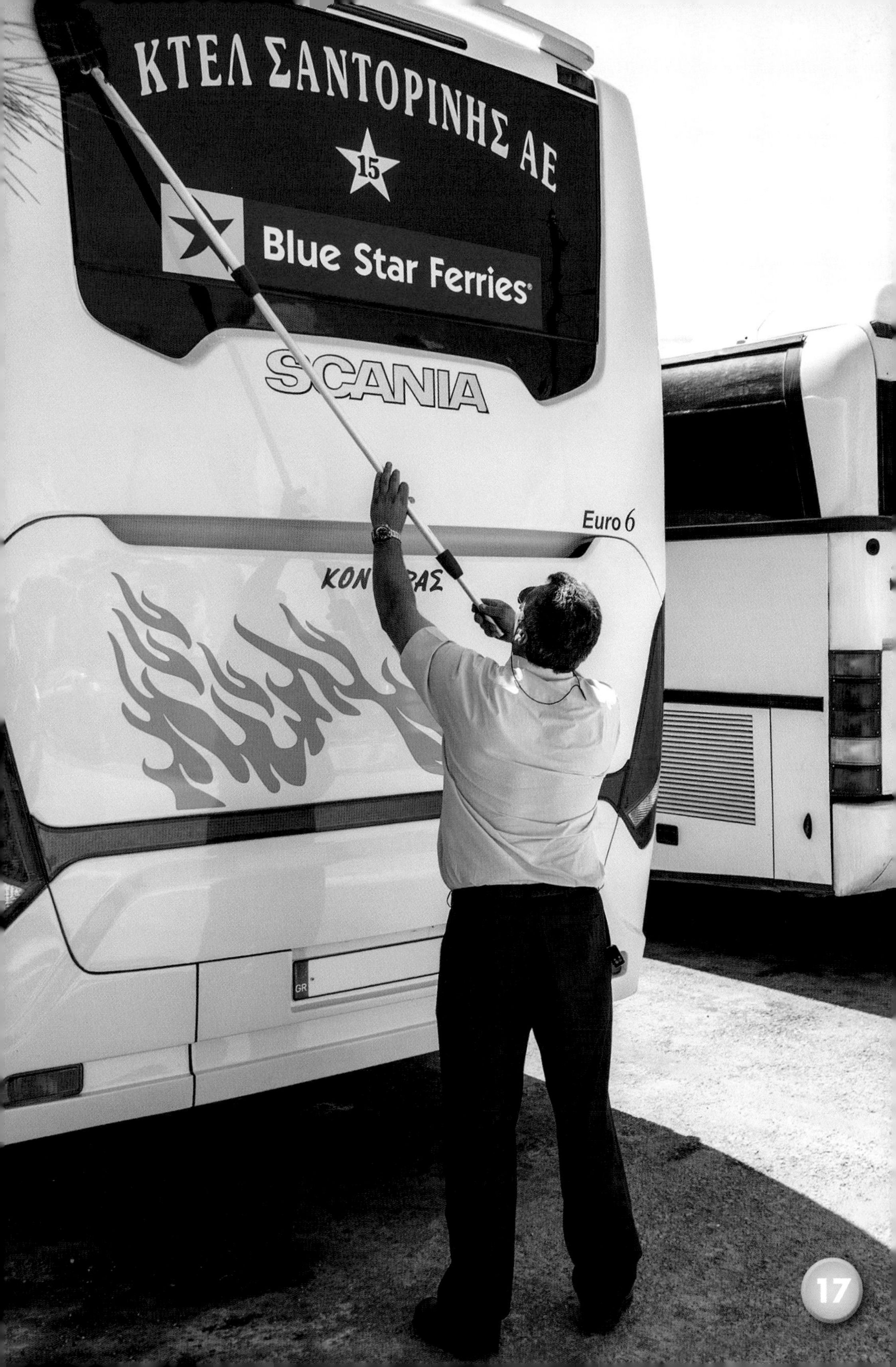
ΚΤΕΛ ΣΑΝΤΟΡΙΝΗΣ ΑΕ
15
Blue Star Ferries
SCANIA
Euro 6

What Makes a Good Bus Driver?

Bus drivers know their routes well. Every stop is important!

Bus Driver Skills

✓ safe drivers   ✓ timely

✓ alert   ✓ friendly

They must be on time. Passengers have places to be!

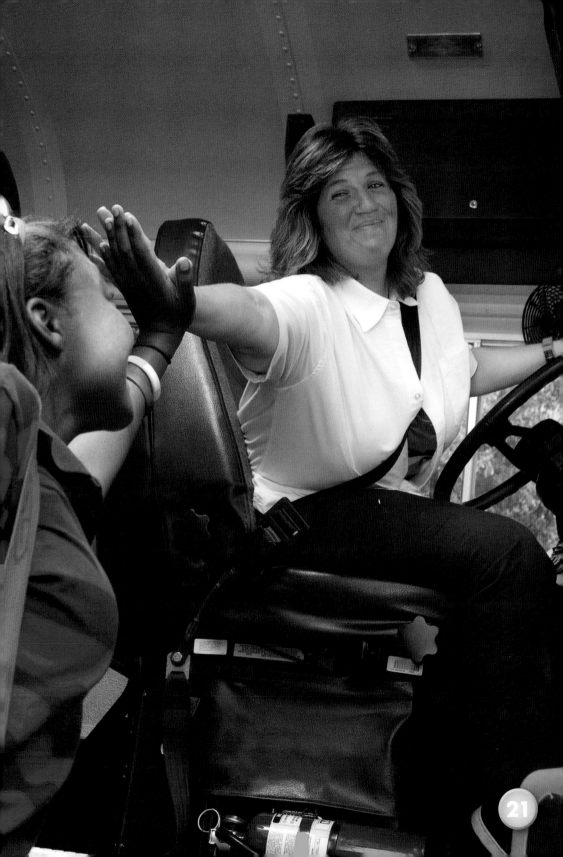

Glossary

fares

money paid to ride the bus

route

a path that is commonly followed

field trips

trips students go on with their class to learn about new things

tours

trips to see and learn about a place

passengers

people who ride in a vehicle to get from one place to another

traffic laws

rules that people must follow on roads and streets

To Learn More

AT THE LIBRARY
Bell, Samantha. *Bus Driver*. Ann Arbor, Mich.:
Cherry Lake Publishing, 2017.

Garrett, Winston. *Let's Ride the School Bus!*
New York, N.Y.: PowerKids Press, 2015.

Murray, Julie. *School Buses*. Minneapolis,
Minn.: Abdo Kids, 2016.

ON THE WEB

Learning more about
bus drivers is as easy
as 1, 2, 3.

1. Go to www.factsurfer.com.

2. Enter "bus drivers" into the search box.

3. Click the "Surf" button and you will see a
   list of related web sites.

With factsurfer.com, finding more information
is just a click away.

Index

buses, 8, 16
cities, 8
clean, 16
drive, 8, 10, 14
fares, 14, 15
field trips, 10
gear, 13
passengers, 12,
    14, 15, 20
people, 10
ride, 4
route, 14, 18
school, 10
skills, 19
stop, 18
tours, 10, 11
towns, 8

traffic laws, 12
work, 8, 10

The images in this book are reproduced through the courtesy of: kali9, front cover, pp. 18-19; DW labs Incorporated, pp. 2-3; lisegagne, pp. 4-5, 6-7; Jim West/ Alamy, pp. 8-9; Werner Dieterich/ Westend61/ SuperStock, pp. 10-11; Michael Folmer/ Alamy, pp. 12-13; Nadir Keklik, p. 13 (steering wheel); Jerry Horbert, p. 13 (stop signs); rSnapshotPhotos, p. 13 (lights); rangizzz, p. 13 (sunglasses); Monty Rakusen/ Alamy, pp. 14-15; Gorelovs, pp. 16-17; Ron Nickel/ Alamy, pp. 20-21; unguryanu, p. 22 (top left); Monkey Business Images, p. 22 (center left); Sergii Rudiuk, p. 22 (bottom left); meowKa, p. 22 (top right); Caron Badkin, p. 22 (center right); Lucky Team Studio, p. 22 (bottom right).